Hidden Music

RALPH DARTFORD

Valley Press

First published in 2021 by Valley Press
Woodend, The Crescent, Scarborough, YO11 2PW
www.valleypressuk.com

ISBN 978-1-912436-68-2
Cat. no. VP0189

A CIP record for this book is available from the British Library.

Cover and text design by Peter Barnfather.
Cover artwork by Pete McKee.
Edited by Emma King.

Printed and bound in Great Britain by
Imprint Digital, Upton Pyne, Exeter.

HIDDEN MUSIC

Ralph Dartford hails from Basildon in Essex, and now lives in West Yorkshire, having got there via Australia, Barcelona and Los Angeles. He was the founding member of influential spoken word collective 'A Firm of Poets', and his first collection of poetry, *Cigarettes, Beer and Love* was published by Ossett Observer Presents in 2013. His next collection, *Recovery Songs*, was published by Valley Press in 2019.

Contents

for Helen Wilkinson

Prelude

'We included everything we wanted to say without saying it.'
– Duke Ellington

Picture this scene. A November night in 1976. I'm a dyslexic boy of twelve years of age living in the new town of Basildon, Essex. I'm sitting alone in the passenger seat of a grey Vauxhall Viva whilst my dad has gone into a pub to meet other men to discuss pigeon racing. He's left me with a bottle of orange pop, a stripy straw and a packet of salted crisps. The radio is still switched on and my sticky fingers twiddle the tuning knob searching for an unknown mystery. Through the tinny speaker I hear people talking in foreign languages; there is static, then loud guitars with angry, nasty, anarchic voices. On and on I go, twisting left and right, right then left. Looking, listening. Outside, rain begins to percuss the roof and windows, brown the streets. Then I find it, the sound. It's shiny and bright. It's joyful, jumpy and new. The discordant melodies moan and converse in secret, instruments argue then laugh with each other. The big beat lifts me, charges me. This is it! I've discovered a language I understand but don't know what it means. I've found the hidden music. Poetry!

Ralph Dartford, Summer 2020

Diminuendo in Blue (live) by Duke Ellington and His Orchestra

Empire

A London summer flexed
her lust to end our October.
In the sweat the wretched flies
raved above us as we listened
to Dusty Springfield sing from
Memphis on your record player.

Occasionally, a sly breeze blew
through our windows – echoes
of a big crowd cheering from
the old Kennington Oval.
A wicket may have been
snatched – a six, crashed.

Cricket.
An English
game gifted
to an Empire.

On the last
afternoon we
were naked on
a bed. Breathless,
weakened and fluid.
We both wanted that
cigarette, but heat ached.

"It's time you went."
"I'm frightened."
"Don't be."

That evening
the storm came,
washing the season.

Albion's radios
were all switched on.

Flies that itched
had now flown and gone.

Son of a Preacher Man by Dusty Springfield

To Recover

In hindsight, he should have
known his days, thrown,
would not settle so far.

Or that there were no truths
to be found in Red Wing boots
or Woody's jangled guitar.

His ascent to razored mountains –
digging a borrowed, reckless scene.
Boys shouting, 'Go, go, go baby!'

Then swallowing bottled beatitude.
The west coast bay shore hymnals,
a summertime of young America.

Man. He could talk a storm,
cause riots in snow domes,
smoke moments down to dust.

Time found him lonesome cold.
Unhitched, frayed on ashen roads.
Snuffed out on powdered Jazz.

But tonight, here, in England's north,
he has tea, sweetened rain, the riddle
of Oxford commas,

and this recovery.

Peace Piece by Bill Evans

Before the Bay of Pigs

Warm beer and rosary beads,
clutched for nothing but comfort.
This buttoned-up man is undone.

Nightly.

He two-
    steps
        the boardwalk

as if dancing to Basie.

Clues thrum his head –
a persistent moth

    that finally
            settles
    on a bicycle wheel

where it spins.

*

The road melt, sticky-backed
June day of 1960.

Riding with Esteban Menotti
to the lighthouse and beyond.

Were the flicked Babe Ruth baseball card
and the driving license nicked from the pages
of his Salinger book in the ecstasy of afterglow?

When they entwined in the singing grass?

And what about that found wallet?

It was nothing.

But Jesus Christ
he was something,
wasn't he?

Legs of muscle,
soft cinnamon kisses,
Spanish brown eyes.

A rock-solid knee trembler
aching to be a man
of his time.
He came,
he went.
That boy.

"Creo que te quiero."

Denim and dimes.

*

Now the bruised
mist shrouds heavy.
Muffling the rollercoaster,
pulling a tarp over the day.

He falls asleep
          on blown popcorn
                    and dreams cheaply
                              of his impossible, starless America.

Of Esteban's infatuation
with the Cubans.

The riddlesome
rendezvous
in Mexico City.

Sofrito by Mongo Santamaria

10.28am Breaking

Every September
I've gone there.

Sometimes it's been sunny
and I've had cold coffee.

All through those times,
I couldn't help myself
from looking up –
couldn't help seeing

the
jumpers

dripping
their stories
into a bitumen book.

Today, it's occasional
showers and I've walked
the long day through.

I've crossed the Brooklyn Bridge –
found the hot grounded Java.

Turned off the morning
breaking news.

Black Swan by Thom Yorke

Considering Lucy

I remember it well.
John Lennon and I were
just putting the dishes away
and wiping the sides down.

The radio was on.
A programme about Border Collies
being the best dogs to prevent
loneliness in the old.

Then, through the kitchen window,
we saw it. A comet or shooting star.
It was in this moment that I realised
we cannot stop falling apart.

Oh! Darling by The Beatles

Soho Twitchers of 1985

Friday cometh the murmuration.
Payday peacocks say farewell to the week.
Flaunt their feathers on Old Compton Street.
Peck the pavements on Dean, Frith and Greek.

Hop the pubs as if they were penguins.
Neck amphetamines and Guinness –
the black on white, the white on black
in praise of Colin MacInnes.

Dance to music that's misunderstood
from New York to Mornington Crescent.
A shop robin spins in Penny Loafers,
a starling threatens the pheasants.

A pop idol swans into Bar Italia.
A Maltese magpie cuts into a cheek.
They flutter and chirp into daylight's gauze,
the young sparrows of Dean, Frith and Greek.

The Sidewinder by Lee Morgan

What I Heard in Sharrow Vale

Now then!

In December 1950
Pablo Picasso
visited Sheffield
for a haircut
and some peace.

It was as cold
as cubism
that day
at Butler's Café.

They say, and I don't know
if it's true, that Pab had
a big old fry-up.

Some even go on to say
that when the plate arrived
the artist made a face
out of the

eggs sausage,
and beans.
A smile of Hendo's Relish.

It's only what some
folk say though
in Sharrow Vale.

Guitar Boogie Shuffle by Frankie Virtue and The Virtues

Tough

Encore of another terrible tour.
He would speed away from Mansfield,

lighting and sound packed and racked
for a week, maybe two. Who knew?

A tough loneliness in cheap hotels –
mornings lost in coffee cups.

It would all start again soon enough –
other bands in other broken towns.

*

Fading the stage to rose red,
triggering oily smoke machines –

he could see her swaying,
raising her hands to mirror-balls.

She's always there, frozen in Paris.
Leatherette and place your bets.

Days of decadence and Rock and Roll.
Days of no caveats and loss of control.

*

She'd told him that he'd got lucky –
that her sweat was set for the drummer.

But tonight she'd take on anyone
on account of her blackening blood.

La vie en rose by Edith Piaf

And Tawdry Days

Excrement-drifting streets pushed
by forty-five-degree winds,
rains from icy syringes.

The nameless boys
encouraged
by the godless men.

Oh, tattoo of youth!

Your journeys to glory
ignite for the last time
in monochrome bedlam.

These sodium songs
that cheer reddened
cacophonies.

The songs that chaperone
death knells – fertilising
history's poppy fields.

Army Dreamers by Kate Bush

Nineteen and the Mermaids

Found after a storm,
by a walker out on his own
after a Christmas lunch
for one, was a sand letter
and three pairs of clogs
which were in truth
unbefitting for terrain
such as this.

He read with keen
interest the swept
italics two or three times,
written with strong fingers
or perhaps a stick or stone.
No wonder he was alone
with his parents, thoughtless
presents and these passions.

He charged the merry wind
to the sly water's edge,
peered at the horizon,
chewed his bottom lip
and tried to light a cigarette
with hotel matches
that laughed
and sizzled at him.

He peeled off his brogues,
tugged the hole in one
sock and loosened his tie.
He pushed a hand through
his hair, skipped into
the surf for life and for joy.
A quartet of delirium in love
with beckoning mermaids.

Fifteen more appear,
ambled from the dunes.
Singing carols and curses,
fed on turkey and time,
drunk on apricot brandy,
primed and ready basted
to contribute to the wonder
of the shoe shop on the beach.

How to Disappear Completely by Radiohead

Sunday in Susan's Room. England, Summer 1982

Outside. Red roses and creosote,
overalls and medium wave. Jimmy
Savile spun the hits from the years.

Inside. We revised geography in our Woolworths
underwear. Motes of pollen swirled in a roll.
We couldn't feel it, but somewhere there was air.

On your radio, war correspondents
predicted the truth of living in scenarios –
the moments of oncoming death.

Then we heard the goads of a twentieth-
century woman. Her patriotic roast beef
anecdotes. A sweet, white wine breath.

Of how we were going to get
some fucking teeth knocked out
if we didn't just listen to her.

That night, the troops mustered and sang
Shoot that poison arrow through my heart
but failed to understand 'Come on Eileen'.

Shipbuilding by Elvis Costello

The Coal Porter

Walking with sand tides
against methane winds.
A man shadowed through
gunmetal blue seeks coal.

There were once days
of counting ways
of how to live,
he'd been told.

Where the young
sang for sixpence,
kissed girls in rock pools
for fool's gold.

Where his mother
sold shells, Oyster
ice creams in front
of Punch's violence.

Waiting for 'Madam
Turner's Tarot'
to turn her cards
to another silent child.

But then the gales
came wilder to paint
a soft green sea black.

Blew them off kilter to Palookaville.

The mansions,

the candy floss shacks.

And now there are no other
days of counting the waves.
The boats twitching the horizon.
Madam Turner's lies.

Only the coal in his sack.

Soulville by Ben Webster

Therapy Room. 4.26pm

Come heavy weather, beware of the rain.
Murder, rape, addiction and grief.
Four chairs silent, reliant upon pain.

Broken, unspoken, bewildered and slain.
Tightened isobars blown by a thief.
Come heavy weather, beware of the rain.

Cast a forecast and bombast them again.
Sow a storm that scatters belief.
Four chairs silent, reliant upon pain.

Surrounded by thunder, light into brain.
Christ alive! They can't get no relief.
Come heavy weather, beware of the rain.

Umbrellas made of paper and cane.
Mercury sinks and rattles the teeth.
Four chairs silent, reliant upon pain.

We're the barometers of a pressure profane.
They sit on us, but what's underneath?
Come heavy weather, beware of the rain.
Four chairs silent, reliant upon pain.

On the Nature of Daylight by Max Richter

St Osyth Bay

If only Archduke Ferdinand
had taken a holiday in St Osyth.
If only we'd stopped Hitler in '36
with a bunch of bloomed white roses.
If only Blair had taken Ecstasy
with Bush in a field of bliss.
If only Lampard's goal had been given
a wife could've been saved with a kiss.
If only George had turned a different corner
he might have been released from all his pain.
If only you'd stop buying a lottery ticket
because your numbers have not come up again.
If only you could give all your small change
to that homeless lass looking up at stars.
If only you'd believe the undisputed truth
because there's lies in them old tarot cards.

A Different Corner by George Michael

Come Sunday

Whilst you scrubbed your kitchen
on Sunday morning Methamphetamine
an old woman tapped at your door.

She'd moved here yesterday –
baked you a pie of apple
and cinnamon.

She did this to say hello.
To show a kindness.

She did this to calm herself
from loneliness and fear.

But you missed her.

Your pumping
headphones shouted
'Jumpin' Jack Flash'
by the Stones.

Your chrysalis glass
and oblivion left her walking

back to a family film.

Her brother was a Nazi.
An SS man at Belsen.
His final breath now taken
to her last interrogation.

And all this happened the night before
she moved her misgivings to your street.

In this dappled, July sunshine;
life. She'll try again tomorrow.

Come Sunday by Duke Ellington and His Orchestra with Mahalia Jackson

In Childhood

Don't step upon the cracks.
For this is where the fingers
lurk that will pull at your sandals,

loosen your buckles and force
you to flail face down onto
the cut glass path.

It's here where they will twist
your ankle, snap it to the moon,
pay the rats to tattoo your bones.

Clicking, they will unscrew your
good leg, let it brittle in the wind
until blackened, bloodless and thin.

Rainbirds by Tom Waits

The Couple

As if weavers on a deadline
they won't engage in eye contact,
tittle tattle, our daily dreams
of a kind revolution.

Here's a prophylactic, a lottery
ticket and twig. The couple build
on a breeze as a prayer decrees
its reason of anywhere but here.

On the banks we wait with worry
about thugs, thieves and Thursday.
The taxing of the poor, how many
eggs she'll eventually lay.

Swans by Prefab Sprout

Begging's Not My Business

She found coins by her pillow.
        Perhaps with current inflation

this was the new rate
        that tooth fairies dispensed.

Downstairs in the kitchen
        she heard the brittle rattle of pans.

A Sunday morning fry-up for two,
        washed down with whiskey in cans.

She'd willingly exchange spent
        pennies for his thoughts

but concluded that punches
        are fiscally just noughts

and crosses to bear.
        The counting of small change.

Up the Junction by Squeeze

On London Bridge I Fell Down and Wept

My ex-wife sitting naked on the bare stone
floor smoking my cigarettes listening
to *The Songs of Leonard Cohen.*

It was the holiest thing that I had ever seen.

*

She told me on night of her return
that she'd been working in Chicago
teaching 'Historical Printing Techniques'.

I knew this to be untrue.

I'd seen her in disguise
serving at the Starbucks
on Charlotte Street
a fortnight before.

I didn't mind that deceit,
just the blueberry muffins
she placed out of reach.

*

She left me because I got too big.
Not in the career sense.
She became childish and cruel,
nicknamed me the 'Room Darkener'.

I refuelled more and more.

*

In her first few days back
in this flat there were incantations,
mumbles, some chanting.

She'd sit on the sofa,
eyes darting.

Perhaps searching
for a mark on the wall.

In the other hours between
not drinking wine in her nakedness
she busied herself by making soup
using odd ingredients from the back
alleys of Kentish Town.

There was this one-sided
conversation of her new plan.

"Fragrant potions would shed pounds off me."

I knew that in the larder
rested an unopened jar
of crunchy peanut butter.

It made my heart beat faster
when I closed my eyes.

In those moments I could feel
her upon me, convincing herself
of a spiritual awakening.

*

Yesterday, though, I was led
into a candlelit living room.

She swapped Cohen for Dylan,
her hair was down.

Wearing one of my old shirts,
her tongue licking thick,
glossy red lipstick.

On the table stood a family sized
bucket of Kentucky Fried Chicken,
bottles of strong, ice cold beer.

She took me by the hand,
waltzed with me to the song
All I Really Want to Do.

It's one of my favourite tirades;
I used to send her the lyrics
in those desperate letters.

I was kissed,
encouraged to lightly
stroke her boned back.

She told me that she loved me,
that she had been a vile liar.
Her ways had to stop.

We went to the curtained bedroom,
sweating pure salt and history.
That song played within us.

*

At dawn, I threw
the chicken away,
the peanut butter.

I walked from Bloomsbury
to London Bridge where I fell
down and wept in the needle rain.

I caught the silent
train to Lewes.

All I Really Want to Do by Bob Dylan

Donny and Marie Stole the Highlights

In a New Town hallway,
opposite the cupboard
that hid a menagerie of coats
with secrets in their pockets,
rested our technology.

Avocado in tone and mutant of trill.
It was the business headquarters
of a family facing the final shrill
of the dirty decade with the optimism
of post-war spivs.

My dad with his greyhound
tips and building site blackmail.
My brother, Joe, hustling fake Donny
Osmond autographs, and me declaring
love to Marie Smith of the fourth form.

We went to the cinema. Our lips chapped
from all the kissing. She fed me up
with someone else's Luncheon Vouchers.
I sold them on to Martin Piper
for Panini stickers plus the usual fee.

But the next Saturday afternoon.
My sister, April, handed me the phone,
all sticky and wet from fairground honeycomb.
'I don't wanna go out with you anymore.
And my mum is coming to see yours!'

Linden Arden Stole the Highlights by Van Morrison

Breathing Lessons

Realisations can choke.
The empty biscuit tin, the final scrape
of butter. The dirty tuppence from the jar.

Breath, when taken deeply,
can dislodge truths that lock.
If only I could exhale

the men who held me down
and entered me that night.
That night they said I was loved.

Hurt by Johnny Cash

A Case of Lulu

It's the dusk of the firefly.
Just after a steaming Dixie storm in the once
upon a time American town of Crystal City, South Texas.

And it's where we catch Lulu. A late forties strawberry blonde
with a red ribbon in her hair, smoking green homegrown
in a beaten-up pink Coupe de Ville of questionable ownership

which she's parked outside a neon-buzzed cantina called
'Billy's Super Rib' that has an outstanding hygiene record,
and that proudly never closes,

where she's worked as a waitress for seven years now,
serving beef and bean burritos to the soundtrack of tinny
Mariachi radio that achingly never ends.

She hasn't much to declare, just the wet dust. The Theremin wind.
The boys that have come and gone on motorcycles and Methadone.
'Hasn't much' has been too much!

So Lulu takes that final drag, flicks the roach out of the window
and pedals the wreck into reverse.

She slams in that old Joni tape that sings
all the way to Newfoundland under
a twinkling, pinprick, roadmap night.

Oh starlight, snow plough and Richard. Oh Canada.

The Last Time I Saw Richard by Joni Mitchell

Woody Guthrie Says

I've sat in circles of addicts and heard
stories of belief and higher powers.
Of Gods of their own understanding
trumping Jesus and a burning bush.

I've never fuelled their fires. I've wept
tears to extinguish suffering, salted
just enough to see me home to bed.
My act of living is a volume of poetry.

But today I saw a man so broken
every step was one towards death.
Kids took photos on their Brownies.
Lord! He was writing his own epitaph.

I boarded the wrong train to glory,
sensed the return of the razored edge.
I exited to rattling thorns of rain, but
tonight, again, I'll surrender to his love.

A Love Supreme, Pt.1: Acknowledgement by John Coltrane

Wisconsin

He speaks to the nation through the night-time
networks. The wants he peddles and needs
are shiny, grimy, repugnant and ugly.

And how will the people die?

He screams for ice cream. The Muslims,
a Chinaman, the lazy of Louisiana.
He'll burn the blood of every creed.

And can you count the people who'll die?

It won't be in a year, next month, tomorrow, but today.
The jewelled old ladies from Queens. The bleached-
out families from Wisconsin shacks.

And can you name the people who died?

This Land is Your Land by Woody Guthrie

Escaping Aleppo

Gripping the trunk, he climbed.
A consumptive, rucksacked boy
high through the whips of the last tree.
Above the town, he read of magic.

He studied books on how to hide.
The clay cities under the desert,
the soft holes through starless nights.
Pages so bright as to vanish his war.

He blew the dust off Harry Houdini, who
died on Halloween, in St Grace's Hospital,
Detroit. A roundhouse to the abdomen.
He questioned other tricks or treats,
the detonation of his belt, and had this
old tree of Aleppo ever borne its fruit?

Jesus Drives a Hyundai

Kings Lynn.
Saturday night late.
The girl's unlaced boots
can't walk in a straight line.
There's a man leering as she
pulls her skirt an inch lower to
the height of her January thighs.

Ipswich.
A bottle smashes
a birthday kiss forever.
A step forward and flinch
to the right and the couple
just might have had a life by
the sea. Grandchildren and love.

Colchester.
An addict ties a red ribbon
tight to find a vein. A cloudy
syringe plunges to black oblivion.
The smile first, then a dealers' panic.
Take his wallet, take his watch. Everything
is collateral in this old land of blood and money.

Norwich.
In a church murdered
by candlelight, the fight fades
and no more the choir will pray.
Driving hard though a winter wind,
he's through the Fens and so far away.
Singing, "I'm through the Fens and so far away."

Jesus Alone by Nick Cave and the Bad Seeds

Pop!

In 1978 only the 'Pop Inn Cafe'
was open on a Sunday.

Warm and lit amongst
the dead of the greengrocer,
baker, the hateful bookmaker
who took all our fathers to the dry
cleaners the afternoon before.

Hidden behind the steamed
windows, there were men
in sideburns and tattoos
chasing the pages of the *News
of the World*. Lighting a fag –
illuminating a saucy vicar's wife.

There was cheese on toast,
Alvin Stardust on the jukebox.
The pinball machine was broken,
the wizard never came to fix it.
Someone even wrote letters
to 'Jim'll'. Once, twice,
three times to nothing.

And its 2020 now.
The 'Pop Inn' a tale
that old men tell other
sons over muesli, eggs
and smashed avocado

before sparking a roll-up,
inhaling deeply to read the titbits
of a saucy vicar's husband

on their iPhones.

Sugar, Sugar by The Archies

From Hoxton Square to Division Street

I'm running behind time when the over-
motivated coked-up Hackney cab driver
arrives all amplified and swinging,
demanding that I walk five hundred
miles, and then five hundred more.

I curse him with anxiety, turn my tired eyes
to other streets and consider the truths
of the imperfect victims of Sheffield,
even those boys born in the sunshine of Leith.

I warm to my theme – a play for today scored
with ancient music. Produced in monochrome,
rehearsed in Bow. Why are we northern folk
regarded tarnished and spiritually poor?

My cab driver turns the volume up.
I leave his door ajar, lurch for my train.
A furnaced steel city song reveals itself.
A song forged from the common people.
Those prone to pallor, those profound of faith.

Common People by Pulp

The Honourable Member

The quick of the fall.
A punch to the heart outside
a hardware store is all it took.

I knew him as a schoolboy,
the way he rubbed dog shit
into a Chinese lad's hair.
He had dreams of war.

Flat on his back now –
crying for his mother.
A woman from Napoli – long gone.
She was of good standing.

I watch from under streetlight.
The knowledge that he'll always be fine.
I think I'll creosote the shed this spring.

Nature Boy by Miles Davis

The Curtain

I'm lost in the Raymond Carver poem.
The one with the boys delivering newspapers –
the coffee cup and how happiness comes
on without any talk of it.

I guess that these days I'm questioning
the dawn and how can I endorse my place.

An old ache has returned. The radio news
with its savage blue lies that promise to get us
back on our feet. Whilst outside our window
a red fox rips hearts open.

Newsroom by Paul Buchanan

Victory to the Miners!

There are indentations within
this chipboard wall from bedposts,
punched sex and addiction.
Takeaway menus in the hallway gloss
over red gas bills. Her birthday cards.

This keyhole is worn.
Busted with burn marks and glue.
There's carved names on the doorframe –
unfinished and uncontested.
Who really loved who?

On the front step, a bottle of milk curdles
sweetly from four days of hot wind, sparrow
pecks and piss. Bags of crisps, chicken
bones and chips stench and crunch
the pavement that wends to the dustbin.

Inside, torn wedding day photos, syringes
and shit. There's a teddy bear with one ear.
The other chewed off through fear. A blood
transfusion in intensive care, and a little
girl lost on the streets. Somewhere.

Between the Wars by Billy Bragg

Hockney and I

He's always been tricks of light, you know.
Los Angeles, the East Yorkshire Wolds.
Still acting out his naughty boy ways.
The bug-eyed, pencil-sharpened schemer.

He sketches here upon his phone.
Caresses the screen, its tweets and tone.
Fingers circle to find birds in a scurry.
We are weeded when living without colour.

But I've worked a wage from stage to ditch.
A weekend wizard to every wise witch.
And if all art mirrors life's mediocrity
then I'm just sleight of hand too, you see.

Northern Sky by Nick Drake

Alcatraz Housing Estate, Basildon

Perhaps once every other summer
there are those sacred hours

when the air, the fragrance and this heat
are all in this singular place.

Sometimes it's hard to touch nostalgia,
but I swear I almost saw you today.

A trimmed rose, a bookmarked
page. Telling me what was for tea.

English Rose by The Jam

Waiting for Geraniums

I work lonesome shifts counting
time. One hour inside, then three
hours outside. Both within this heat.

I twitch from home-assembled
tables. There is French filtered coffee,
English anxiety, cadged cigarettes.

There are other people who have
other passions. I'm aware nosy
neighbours talk in their kitchens.

But I need this. That beyond my rosy
garden fence rises a fertile rebellion.
A blossomed siren and nightshade.

Summertime by Ella Fitzgerald and Louis Armstrong

Whilst Reading Anne Tyler

I was something else
sometime ago.

I know that if I wanted I could
climb the twelve stairs,

open the battered brown case and pull
out that day on Venice Beach.

The photo with the Arab skateboarding,
playing saxophone – digging a scene.

I was leather-jacketed, Kerouac, shades.
Legs crossed on rail tracks preparing my cheap

reasons for the years. Needle, nose and numb.
I'm sometime else now. Someone hence.

Let's Get Lost by Chet Baker

The Vote

Thursday afternoon and I'm walking home.
Not far, just down the hill from the campaign.
Buttershaw, South Bradford. The north.

Weather hard and splintered. A mist of mustard.
The traffic is angry, the streets the colour of beer.
It was in these moments that I knew it was over.

The woman who said it was the immigrants.
The boy who told me, "Piss off back to London!"
The weak coffee, the stale biscuits of yesterday.

I sat and counted hours. Hunted Twitter for clues.
But I saw it in that rain, the arched backs of old men.
Yes. I saw it in the rain. The faces accepting of lies.

Here's Where the Story Ends by The Sundays

Being There

And to be honest, I can't even remember
her name. She was Spanish, that's for sure.
From the islands, or was it Seville?

So anyway, I met her at a party, or did I?
No actually, a friend set us up. I recall
it went on for a while. The summer of 1984.

She was an au pair, maybe a student.
Lived in Streatham, maybe Kennington.
She liked to walk hand in hand by the river.

A first kiss in Piccadilly, a film in Leicester Square.
But it could have been in St Martins Lane.
It was Peter Sellers in 'Being There'.

We slept in a bed on the Charing Cross Road.
A Peabody flat. A private, curtained quietness.
I left her for a florist from Basildon.

Looking back, I don't know why I ran away.
Perhaps it was beauty, maybe a fear of touch.
Marita was her name. The loveliness of the sun.

Reminisce by Dexys Midnight Runners

Older

Yes. Let's take it!

Let's steal this day now as if delinquent,
sugar-raged, gob-stopper-sucking kids.

Let's run through these blue corn-flowered
meadows and tie daisies into each other's
long gone, wild black curly hair.

Let's hold hands, skip and scream into it.

Yes. Come on!

New Grass by Talk Talk

Acknowledgements

This collection was edited with extreme care by the wonderful Emma King.

The poem 'Nineteen and the Mermaids' first appeared in my debut collection, *Cigarettes, Beer and Love*, which was published by 'Ossett Observer Presents'.

The poem 'What I Heard in Sharrow Vale' first appeared in the anthology *A Firm of Poets: Holding Your Hand Through Hard Times* which was published by 'Ossett Observer Presents'.

The poem 'Waiting for Geraniums' first appeared in the anthology *Beyond the Storm* which was published by 'Write Out Loud'.

'Hidden Music – A Playlist by Ralph Dartford' is available on Apple Music and Spotify.

With grateful thanks to the following:

Arts Council England for financial support in the development of this project.

Chris Jones and the creative writing department at Sheffield Hallam University.

Jill Adam, Dan Mallaghan, Pete McKee, Ed Cooper, Nick Jones, Jonny Syer, Anne and Richard Lee, Elizabeth Grant, Phil Burdett, Leonie Hilliard, Sarah and Paul Maybury, Becky Swain, Emma Wilkinson, Liam O'Shea, Jacqui Wicks, Michael Ball and John Bulley.